For the Dell family: Andy, Sylvia,
Alastair, Kathryn, Olivia and Georgie,
who made a new family – M.H.

For Jessie, Lola, Lenny and Lucie Lorne – R.A.

JANETTA OTTER-BARRY BOOKS

Text copyright © Mary Hoffman 2010
Illustrations copyright © Ros Asquith 2010
The rights of Mary Hoffman to be identi ed as the Author and of
Ros Asquith to be identi ed as the Illustrator of this Work have been
asserted by them in accordance with the Copyright, Designs and Patent Act, 1988.

First published in Great Britain in 2010 by
Frances Lincoln Children's Books, 74-77 White Lion Street,
London, N1 9PF
www.franceslincoln.com

A catalogue record for this book is available from the British Library.

ISBN: 978-1-84507-999-4

Illustrated with watercolours

Set in Green

Printed in China
7 9 8 6

THE GREAT BIG BOOK OF FAMILIES

Where am I? Can you find me every time you turn a page? And can you find out my name?

Mary Hoffman
Illustrated by Ros Asquith

F

FRANCES LINCOLN
CHILDREN'S BOOKS

Once upon a time most families in books
looked like this –

One daddy, one mummy, one little boy, one little girl,

But in real life, families come in
all sorts of shapes and sizes.

one dog   and one cat.

In this book are a lot of families living
in different ways. Perhaps there's one
that looks like yours?

FAMILIES

Lots of children live with their mummy and daddy,

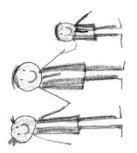

but lots of others live
with just their daddy

or just their mummy.

Some live with their grandma and grandpa.

Some children have two mummies or two daddies.

And some are adopted or fostered.

WHO'S IN YOUR FAMILY?

Some people have lots of brothers and sisters...

great GRANNY JANE   GRANNY ESME   GRAMPA BILL   granma SUZIE   granpa JOE   great granma EVELYN

AUNTY JANE   AUNTY FLO   UNCLE BOB   UNCLE ABDUL   AUNTY AMY   SISTER MIA   AUNTY SADIE

My Family

and uncles and aunties...

and cousins...

and grandmas and grandpas.
And even great grandmas
and great grandpas.

But some people have really
small families. You can be a
family with just two people.

HOMES

People live in all sorts of homes...

Some small families live in big houses.
And some big families live in tiny flats.

HOMELESS

And some people can't find
anywhere to live.

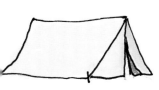

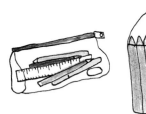

SCHOOL

Most children go to school.

But some are
taught at home.

And some just won't go to school.

But I've been to school already. I went YESTERDAY

Others are too young to go to school.

In some families everyone has a job.

In others only one person goes out to work.

Some parents work from home.

And some can't get a job at all.

HOLiDAYS

Some families go on exotic holidays,

and some stay closer to home.

Some visit families in other countries.

You don't need to pack EVERYTHING

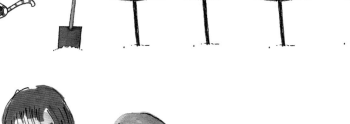

And others go on day trips.

Not all families can afford a holiday. But most people get some time off from work. Even a weekend at home can be a little holiday.

FOOD

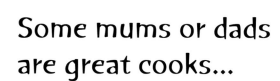

AIKEN DRUM — FINE MEATS SINCE 1896

TOM the PIPER'S SON TAKE~AWAY

MENU

Miss Muff...

Some mums or dads are great cooks...

Others prefer to buy ready-made meals.

BURGERS 4 US

Most families get their food
from shops or markets.

But some people grow their own.

CLOTHES

Some children get new clothes.

Others have hand-me-downs...
Or their clothes come from charity shops.

Some families dress up for special occasions.

But some like to wear jeans all the time.

And some dress any way they please.

PETS

Some people believe their pets are members of their family.

And some pets think they're very important family members.

Some people even look like their pets.

Is a teddy a pet?

Some families can't have pets - but it doesn't stop them dreaming...

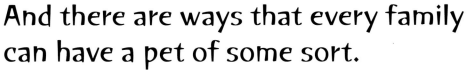

And there are ways that every family can have a pet of some sort.

Am I a pet?

SNAIL RACE

Birthdays are fun, but some families
make more fuss about them
than others.

And then there's Christmas, Divali, Eid,
Hanukkah, Weddings, Christenings,
Bar and Bat Mitzvahs...
Chinese New Year...

Whatever you celebrate in your family,
there are usually some special traditions.

What are we celebrating?

EVERYTHING!

HOBBiES

In some families everyone has the same hobby.

In others, everyone likes doing different things...

TRANSPORT

Some families walk everywhere –
to the shops, to school,
to the doctor...

CARRY!

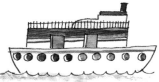

COUGH

Others get about in big cars,

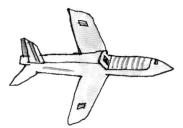

or on bicycles...

Or riding something else...

FEELINGS

In some families everyone shares their feelings.

Other people are more shy. Or perhaps they just like to keep their feelings to themselves.

PRIVATE

Sometimes not everyone in the family feels the same way about things.

And feelings can change quickly.

Have you ever tried to make a family tree?

Sometimes you don't have to go back far to find bits of family who have come from other countries.

And if your mum or dad lives with a new partner,

you might have to make a whole new set of branches.

So families can be big, small, happy, sad, rich, poor, loud, quiet, cross, good-tempered, worried or happy-go-lucky.

Most families are all of these
things some of the time.

What's yours like
today?